FREE SPEECH IN THE CHURCH

KARL RAHNER

FREE SPEECH
IN
THE CHURCH

SHEED AND WARD
LONDON AND NEW YORK

FIRST PUBLISHED 1959
SHEED AND WARD LTD.
33 MAIDEN LANE
LONDON W.C.2
AND
SHEED AND WARD INC.
64 UNIVERSITY PLACE
NEW YORK 3

NIHIL OBSTAT: ADRIANUS VAN VLIET,
S.T.D. CENSOR DEPUTATUS
IMPRIMATUR: E. MORROGH BERNARD
VIC. GEN.
WESTMONASTERII, DIE 26a OCTOBRIS,
1959

The *Nihil Obstat* and *Imprimatur* are a
declaration that a book or pamphlet is
considered to be free from doctrinal or
moral error. It is not implied that those
who have granted the *Nihil Obstat* and
Imprimatur agree with the contents,
opinions or statements expressed.

This book is a translation of *Das freie Wort in der Kirche*,
published by Johannes-Verlag, Einsiedeln.

This book is set in 10 on 11 pt. Linotype Baskerville

*Made and printed in Great Britain by
William Clowes and Sons, Limited, London and Beccles*

CONTENTS

FREE SPEECH IN THE CHURCH

This subject is simply a subdivision of a far wider general topic—the question of the position and function of the laity within the Church, both in the general context of Catholic Action, and in the light of the individual Christian's responsibility for the Church's mission today and the way he co-operates in it. Now, any serious consideration of a matter of one's rights must turn inevitably into a discussion of the duties that lie behind the rights. When the subject under discussion is the individual layman's right to express his own opinion within the Church, then this resolves itself ultimately into a demand that the individual layman shall become aware, not so much of any privilege he may have in this matter, as of his duty to feel a personal responsibility for the Church's official activity.

I should like to approach my subject by way of a slight detour, beginning with the question as to whether there is, might be, or ought to be, any such thing within the Church as a "public opinion"—a phrase used, incidentally, by the late Pope Pius XII.

Even in the secular domain of state, society and the community of nations, public opinion is a highly problematical thing. It is not easy to define; it is frequently guided, and distorted, by powers that are very far from "public"—in fact is often "made" by the State itself. It is subject to all the shortsightedness and the blind passions of the masses and the "spirit of the age". Nor is it clear at first sight why the opinions of a large number of people, of "the public", should be sounder or better for the people and the State as a whole than the opinions of a few; unless one is prepared to cherish the optimistic view that there are more wise men than fools in the world, and that the celebrated "man in the street" is a model of wisdom and probity. Nevertheless, clearly such a thing as public opinion exists in the lives of states and peoples; it has its particular function to play in them, and it must be taken into account by a government when it makes its decisions.

Is there anything corresponding to this in the life of the Church—and, furthermore, should there be? Certainly not, as far as the actual phrase "public opinion" is concerned. This phrase has never been known before in the history of the Church—not even in the days when the reality was playing a part in the lives of states and cities. But a thing can be there, even when it has no name: a new concept can be tacked on to an old reality. Now, there is no reason why the new concept should bring into disrepute the old reality to which it has attached itself; and furthermore, the new word may make the old reality clearer, and bring out its significance both theoretically and practically. But at the same time it is obvious that an idea like the present one, which has been taken from the secular side of life—indeed, is typically modern in its derivation—must be used carefully and in a merely analogous sense when it is applied in the quite different sphere of the sacred. However, if it is true that there are ultimately no concepts in the sphere of religion which do not finally derive from this earth; if the Church herself is "visible", possessing an aspect comprehensible in human terms, indeed, even a law akin to a secular code, although this fact in no way militates against her heavenly origin; if Catholic theology has always held firmly to the principle that the visible aspect of the Church can and must be described "analogously" in terms of the human law; then the mere secular origin of the concept of public opinion cannot be a reason for us not to enquire into the possibility of "public opinion" within the Church.

At first sight it might seem that such a thing as public opinion would be utterly impossible in the Catholic Church. Not that anyone with the least acquaintance with Church history, in both its holy and its unholy aspects, could deny the actual fact of its existence and activity within the Church. It goes without saying that the decisions of the Church are made by the men in the Church, even though their human activities are held in the grasp of the divine Spirit. Clearly, too, these men, notwithstanding the leading and prompting of the Holy Spirit, will behave—for both good and ill—as children of their age. Nor can it be gainsaid that to be a child of one's age is to be influenced, consciously or unconsciously, by the public opinion of one's age. This remains true, even when a churchman imagines himself to be defending the rights and teachings of God and the Church by braving public opinion and acting in diametrical opposition to it. In such a case a man can in fact be in a state of dependence —sometimes fatal dependence—upon public opinion: God and the truth can often remain remarkably remote from parties formed in such a way. In short: The mere fact of the existence of a public opinion within the Church will be questioned by no one. But not everything that exists within the Church has a right to exist, when judged by the Church's true nature and purpose; so that it is still quite possible for anyone to question the *right* of this public opinion to exist, even though it does in fact exist. We might say, for instance, "Public opinion is one of the ways in which the people's will expresses itself in secular society. In a democratic state the people's will governs the decisions made by the Government, and for this reason public opinion has a right to exist and to be respected there. But is this so within the Church? The Church's authority comes from the grace of God, not from the people. It derives ultimately from a divine ordinance, not from a popular election. The laws governing her behaviour are grounded in an unchanging, everlasting constitution granted her by our Lord himself. Essentially, for all her historical development, and though involved in so many ways with the external forces which determine secular history, she is not a product of the changing forces of this secular history but something founded once and for all by God himself, to last until the end of time. The ultimate, decisives forces behind her activity, in the varying conditions of history in which she lives, derive

4

not from men but from the Spirit who has been promised her as the everlasting vital principle of all she does. What place is there, then, for public opinion in such a society?"

And yet there can and should be such a thing as public opinion within the Church. I shall try to show why this must be so later. For the moment it will be sufficient to support this assertion by a reference to the Church's teaching authority. In an address to those taking part in an International Catholic Press Congress (reported in the *Osservatore Romano* of 18 February, 1950), the late Pope Pius XII said:

Public opinion plays a part in every normal society of human beings . . . wherever there is no expression of public opinion, above all, where it has been ascertained that no public opinion exists, then one is obliged to say that there is a fault, a weakness, a sickness, in the social life of that area. . . . Finally, I should like to add a word about public opinion within the fold of the Church—about things that can be left open to discussion, of course. Only people who know little or nothing about the Catholic Church will be surprised to hear this. For she too is a living body, and there would be something missing from her life if there were no public opinion within her, a defect for which pastors as well as the faithful would be responsible. . . .

First, a few reflections by way of commentary on these words spoken by the Church's supreme teacher. The words themselves come from a speech made not about the subject of this essay, but about the nature of public opinion and the need for it in the secular sphere of states and societies, and it is only in the closing section of the address that the subject of this essay is briefly mentioned. But there is no mistaking its assertion of the need for a public opinion within the Church, and its justification of the existence of such public opinion. Any denial of such an activity within the Church is said to be based on an insufficiency, or even a complete absence, of knowledge, about the Church. The existence of a public opinion is justified by the fact that the Church is a society of human beings and that human societies essentially involve public opinion. Any attempt to stifle it would be a mistake, for which both clergy and laity would be held responsible. We must not, of course, overstate the binding power of these words of the Pope's, made in a speech to a congress which was not even published in the Church's official organ, the *Acta Apostolicae Sedis*. We should not ascribe to them a doctrinal authority to which they have no claim. In addresses like this the Pope does not normally intend to settle controversial questions, but rather, in his capacity of ordinary teacher of the Church, to re-emphasize truths which seem to him self-evident and beyond argument. But it is precisely because of this that the Pope's words are of such interest. Looking at the thing from the historical point of view, it would indeed be fair to say that fifty years ago, at about the time of Pius X's Syllabus, such a statement—i.e., the unhesitating admission, as something self-evident,

6

of the existence (and the fully justified existence) of a public opinion within the Church—would have seemed far less indisputable. In fact, one would hardly have expected it then from the lips of a pope. Not that Christian truth changes with changes in its enemies; but inevitably, the front on which the Church has to defend that truth must change as new aspects of this unchanging truth, whose plenitude she always possesses, emerge more fully into her own consciousness. Thus, in an age of liberalism and scientific "freedom" and so on, the emphasis had to be laid on the God-given nature of the Church's teaching authority. In an age of totalitarian states, when individuality is suppressed and "ideology" supplied, the Church has to delimit her position more clearly, to prevent her own character and nature from being confused with those of a totalitarian state. She will now have to come down more firmly on the side of the individual's responsibility and freedom both in his secular and his religious life. She will have to say, for example—as she has not said in so many words before—that there is and should be such a thing as public opinion within the Church, thereby making it clear that the Church is not a totalitarian religious state, no matter what so many people outside the Church may think and say to the contrary.

What sort of a thing is public opinion, as it exists within the Church? In its secular sense "public opinion" includes all the manifestations of the mind and will of the people composing a given society, in so far as these opinions and wishes are, on the one hand, shared by the majority of the people—i.e., are not entirely individual—and, on the other, do not find direct expression through legally constituted channels —such as Parliament and so on. One might therefore be tempted to speak of a public opinion as existing within the Church whenever the views and aspirations of her members develop and find expression, not under the leadership and authority of the Hierarchy but, in the first place at least, side by side with the functions of these "official" powers of the Hierarchy. But this would still be too wide a conception of the matter. For there are in fact in the Catholic idea of the Church certain elements whose embodiment is in the "Church taught" but which nevertheless cannot be included under the heading of "public opinion" within the Church, even though they are common knowledge to all the Catholic laity. The Church's life is sustained not only by the initiative, orders or instructions of ecclesiastical authority, but also, though still under the direction of the Hierarchy, by the charisma of the Holy Spirit, who can breathe upon whomsoever he will in the Church—even the poor, the children, those who are "least in the Kingdom of God"—and infuse his own impulses into the Church in ways that no one can foretell. The "Church taught" has its own understanding of the Faith, its own kind of "infallibility"—in the sense that not only the teaching Church but the "Church taught", as a whole, will always remain within the orbit of divine truth, safe under the power of the Holy Spirit. All those manifestations of strictly supernatural powers and gifts and inspirations, which the Holy Spirit, soul of the Church, is always infusing into God's holy people, are better kept out of what must always be in certain respects the secular idea of "public opinion"; they belong to a higher level of existence than anything this idea usually implies. Nor, for this reason, shall I make any reference in what follows to that freedom of speech which especially characterizes those—mystics and others —who have a special mission from the Holy Spirit or in any way are endowed with a special charism. A subject so important would need separate treatment.

But when all this has been excluded, there is still place in the Church for what can truly be called public opinion. Divine though the Church may be in origin—in her constitution and doctrine, her sacraments and her law—she has an earthly existence too: she has her own *jus humanum*, forms of spirituality, liturgy, care of souls, moral behaviour, administration, societies, organizations, etc., which to some extent, though not exclusively, express the fluctuating, predominantly natural conditions of the day. The Church has always to be adapting her actual existence to contemporary conditions, and these, often far removed from her direct influence, are simply so many "facts", which she must take into account. But it is not always an easy matter to know what in fact are these conditions which form the life and work of the Church. They are very often not simply "facts", but are things made up of the desires, feelings, emotions, worries, and so on, of

9

human beings—of human beings who *could* no doubt be different from what they are, but who are in fact what they are now. What they are now is in many cases the result of free choice by men who "theoretically" (but only "theoretically") could have come to different decisions; but these other decisions could not in all cases be dictated to them.

Moreover, all these "preconditions" are extraordinarily varied and many-sided; they change with the people concerned, with time and place; the changes may take place very quickly, frequently seeming to contradict each other; in fact, they often do so. In short, knowledge of these preconditions to which the life of the Church has to adapt itself is no easy matter, but something to be struggled for and won over and over again. It is here that public opinion within the Church has its true field of activity. From this point of view it is simply the manifestation of the actual situation, which the Church leaders have to be familiar with and take into account—and they can only do this through the people who are living in the situation, who have to live their lives in it as Christians and members of the Church, and thus work out their salvation. Public opinion within the Church, one may therefore say, exists to make plain what people in the Church are really feeling, so that the Church leaders can take account of this in their own action. As has been said above, the "situation" includes a great deal that is the result of voluntary activity and voluntary decisions. A particular Church ordinance or custom *can* be felt in this way or that.

But it is important to know how it is *actually*
felt. For instance, it is theoretically possible for
the liturgy for Holy Saturday to be celebrated
with the utmost piety in the morning, the wor-
shippers overlooking the fact that it is actually
still Saturday morning and not the Easter vigil.
But the kind of thing the clergy need to know is
whether people *do* in fact feel this way about it,
or whether they simply will not do so, even with
good (though not absolutely compelling) grounds
for such action. And in matters of free choice
men's thoughts and feelings should not be pre-
scribed for them. The way people actually feel
about such things must be taken into account as
the "situation" in which the official Church must
take her appropriate action. This may seem a
fairly obvious thing to say, but like many other
obvious things it is often overlooked in practice.
Public opinion is thus one of the means whereby
the Church's official leaders, who need human
aid as well as divine, get to know something
about the actual situation within which, and
taking due account of which, they are to lead
and guide the people. They need to know how
people are thinking and feeling, what they have
set their hearts and wishes on, what their problems are, what they find difficult, in what respects
their feelings have changed, where they find the
traditional answers or rulings insufficient, what
they would like to see changed (even if the
change is not strictly necessary), and so on. The
greater the number of people involved, the more
complex their relationships, the more diverse
their mentalities, the more difficult it is to

obtain this knowledge of the situation, and, therefore, the greater the need for a public opinion.

In a sense there has always been a kind of
public opinion within the Church. All the
"movements" that have taken place in the course
of the Church's history are in the last resort so
many precursors of the development and final
emergence of this kind of public opinion, even
though they were of course more than that.
Nevertheless the phrase "public opinion" should,
in the strict sense, perhaps only be applied to
those cases where individuals, believing themselves to be the mouthpieces of a hitherto un-
expressed point of view, come out in public and
address the masses as publicists, by way of books,
newspapers and public speeches, and so give expression to public opinion and at the same time
help to create it. This situation is only possible
and necessary—at any rate in the secular sphere
—where, as recently, there is a large mass of
people involved, making the analysis of the situation difficult. Only in such conditions does it
become necessary for individual opinions, for
what seem at first sight no more than individual
wishes and aspirations, to be made known to the
general public, that their reaction may determine
whether it is simply a case of the insignificant
views of an individual or whether something
more is involved. In general, therefore, we can
only speak of a "public opinion" when we can
observe the public's reaction to the views and
attitudes of an individual. But if the situation
can only be satisfactorily known in this way,
then it will be necessary, or at least useful, to

give public opinion a chance to develop, by allowing the individual to address the general public. The fact that this is true in Church matters too means that to a certain extent the individual within the Church must be allowed to address the Church community in general as a publicist—not only to make direct representations to the Hierarchy. The authorization or right to do this is not in the last analysis the same as the "democratic" right to express any wish or idea of no matter what kind; from the point of view of the Hierarchy it is simply a useful, and in certain circumstances a necessary, way of getting to know the actual situation. To put it rather frivolously, it allows the individual to talk his head off occasionally, so that one can judge from the way others react whether he is really saying anything of any general concern. Thus, in so far as this is the only way in which the official Church leaders can obtain adequate knowledge of the situation—and today this is very largely the case—to that extent they must allow and indeed encourage the kind of "publicity" that leads to the growth and expression of public opinion. This expression and formation of public opinion cannot in all or even the majority of cases be the effect of guidance and inspiration by the Holy Spirit, or any intelligence superior to the individual's, as is often too optimistically supposed in the secular sphere. Its justification is simply that this is the sole means of discovering what is really going on. If there is any real desire to know the current situation—spiritual, psychological, social, etc.—then Catholics must be allowed (within the limits already laid down) to talk their heads off. Anyone who thinks today he really knows what is going on, without the aid of this means of information, will very often find himself to be most lamentably mistaken. From this point of view, public opinion is the means—a useful and, in these days, to some extent an indispensable means—whereby the Church authorities can get an all-round view of the actual situation. It is well to remember that in the sphere in which this public opinion has a part to play, Church authorities have no gift of infallibility, however much they may be helped and supported by the Holy Spirit. It is always possible to make mistakes, to shilly-shally, to lag far behind the contemporary historical situation—all these things are possible. The clergy possessing official jurisdiction within the Church often have, it is true, a wider view of the real condition of the world and of men's spiritual and intellectual life as a result of their independent position, their remoteness from the pressures of secular activity, their deeper roots in Church tradition. Yet it is also true that they are not infrequently in danger, for the same reasons, of knowing only a limited, merely "clerical" and traditionally sheltered segment of real life and the real position. If they do not allow the people to speak their minds, do not, in more dignified language, encourage or even tolerate, with courage and forbearance and even a certain optimism free from anxiety, the growth of a public opinion within the Church, they run the risk of directing her from a soundproof ivory tower, instead of straining their ears to catch the voice of God, which can also be audible within the clamour of the times.

The above should not only have made clear the meaning of, and the need for, a public opinion within the Church, but also the real subject of this essay—the individual's, and above all the layman's, right to free speech within the Church, which we have already been discussing. This freedom is an essential part of any public opinion, and thus shows up its fundamental difference from the kind of opinion allowed in totalitarian states. This means that the freedom of the individual must by no means be regarded as being restricted to a merely private sphere, with no bearing on the community life of the Church: on the contrary, it has a real place in her public life.

Now that this has been established, we can go on to the more difficult question of the limitations that are to be set to this public opinion, and also the concrete forms it can take in actual practice. It is clear, to begin with, that there can be no discussion of anything that comes into conflict with the Church's dogma and her divinely willed constitution, *juris divini*. Even democracies give no place or recognition to aspirations that deny their own essential nature. The only proper objects of public opinion within the Church are Church matters. An ever-watchful eye is kept on these by priests and theologians, who have long since developed the proper organs for exerting their authority—censorship, the supervision of teaching activities within the

Church, official Church pronouncements and so on—but it must be remembered in this connection that there is always a strong tendency to narrow down far too closely the range of what parts of the Faith can legitimately be discussed. Any such narrowing-down does not in fact help to keep the Faith strong and secure; instead, discussion about the questions concerned drifts far beyond the general Catholic public into regions much harder to keep an eye on, and "cryptogam" heresies[1] arise. Thus a certain degree of freedom of public opinion is necessary even in questions of theology, and the Church has in fact always insisted that she wishes to preserve this freedom and a free exchange of views between the various schools. It would also be a mistake to recognize the right of this freedom to exist only in those cases where it has already to a certain extent been expressly acknowledged by the Church's teaching office, i.e., when old scholastic problems are being treated for the nth time and freedom to discuss them has been expressly given to the parties concerned. The same freedom must also be allowed when questions are being raised and views expressed for which there is no previous guarantee that such and such a comment may be made, or even such and such a subject discussed. In these cases, of course, i.e., when a real theological issue is at stake which has not been decided once and for all by the Church's teaching authority, and when the views

---

[1] Cf. "Ein Gestaltwandel der Häresie", in K. Rahner, *Gefahren im heutigen Katholizismus*, Johannes Verlag, Einsiedeln, 1950, series *Christ Heute*.

put forward cannot be accepted in advance as being at least "safe" (*tuta*), the Church's teaching authority can naturally and quite justifiably make clear to the Catholic public generally that some particular opinion has gone beyond the bounds of what is permissible. But even in these cases it should be assumed—unless there is proof to the contrary—that the theologian concerned has acted in good faith in making use of his *right* to present his views to the general Catholic public. Such a theologian has in the last analysis only performed the function of public opinion as outlined above. He has given the Church officials the opportunity of acquainting themselves with the spiritual currents of their time (which would still be there, even if the offending expressions of them had never been made) and of clarifying their own attitude to them. It is very seldom that the Church's teaching authority is simply called upon to repeat platitudes, which any theologian might be expected to know all about anyway. In any case, theologians who have expressed their views in a clear and honest fashion tend to be affected far more deeply by such negative reactions than do those who put forward the same views, or far "worse" ones, "cryptogamically", and the former should therefore be treated with all the courtesy that befits an honourable opponent in a spiritual battle, even when he is the "loser". And once the spiritual authority has spoken, the persons not affected should refrain from pointing the finger of scorn at those under censure, as if they themselves always knew better. The class of persons that always know better seldom contribute any-thing towards a solution of the problems which have brought the others to grief. The limits to be set in actual concrete cases to the free expression of opinion within the Church will always be to a certain extent a matter of judgement, and the last word in such cases must lie with the Church authorities. Anyone who has spent any time studying Church history will readily agree that again and again—and this is quite consonant with the infallibility of Church doctrine and the support given to the pastoral office by the Holy Ghost—these limits have been set a little too narrowly. There is no need for any examples of this to be mentioned here. Thus public opinion can also perform the useful function of allowing a frank and sincere discussion of the actual limits of public opinion. There is another point worth noting about these theological questions: the more the theological debates are of a professional scientific kind, pursued for the benefit of a narrow specialized public, the more remote the danger becomes of any undesirable influence affecting the vast mass of the laity through this kind of free discussion: the more "academic", in fact, the discussion becomes, the less cause for suspicion and alarm is there in the growth of a limited expression of general opinion. It is true that today, when people find it so easy to hear about every type of question, and like discussing everything under the sun, it is more difficult than it used to be to separate this academic "forum" from the open market of public opinion. Nevertheless, even today it can still be useful to ask whether or not the right moment has in fact arrived for saying or writing something which at another time would be rightly regarded as out of place and rightly call forth a justified reaction from the Church authorities.

In other questions which do not affect, or do not directly affect, the Church's unchanging deposit of faith and her divinely ordained constitution, but are concerned with the *jus humanum* in the Church, her varying practices in the matter of the liturgy, the care of souls, politics, etc., public opinion has a still more vital function to perform within the Church, and hence a still greater right to freedom. At this level any form of "top secret" government would be a really great danger. It is true, of course, that in these matters too the authority of the Church has the last word, and when something is made binding or is forbidden it is simply part of the layman's duty to obey these ordinances and prohibitions. It is also his duty to see that not only the form but also the content of these ordinances and prohibitions (i.e., what is "meritorious" in them) is not discussed publicly in such a way that their observance is vitiated. But it seems necessary to add here that it by no means follows that all discussion of the appropriateness and opportuneness of existing ordinances, practices and so on in the Church should be for this reason ruled out, or carried on, so far as the general public is concerned, behind closed doors. Today, for instance, there can be open discussion as to whether there would be some point in a reform of the Breviary, or even whether there should be a modification of the Mass itself. Can there be any question that this could have taken place decades ago, even though permission for such a discussion—if only unofficial permission—had not expressly encouraged people to embark on it? Would it have been such a bad thing if a few words could have been found occasionally in Catholic newspapers on the subject of the awful complexity of the rules about fasting before Holy Communion, which have not always seemed to preserve the real spirit of this ordinance of the Church? Could not the housing and dress and customs of the various orders be discussed more frankly and openly (in the appropriate journals —which does not by any means mean all of them) than has been the case for a long time now, despite the fact that everyone realizes that a good deal of discussion and reform is needed in this matter? Are there not large groups of people amongst what is on the whole a fairly loyal body of laymen who privately deplore many of the educational methods in use in Catholic insti-tutes and monastic establishments and yet never say a word about it in public—and never will, wrongly imagining that they never may? The fact is that reforms of this kind naturally often need the pressure of public opinion if they are not to be stifled by tradition. Even in the higher reaches of the Church, people can believe that all is well because no complaints and no wishes for any sort of change have been heard, or be-cause if they have they seem to be simply isolated views with no weight of public opinion behind them. The examples mentioned above, it should be added, are of a purely arbitrary kind; nevertheless they may suffice to illustrate what is meant by saying that in this sphere public opinion within the Church should have a wide and not too narrowly circumscribed field of activity.

Views about the limits to be set to the expressions of this public opinion and the forms it should take will naturally vary considerably when it comes to actual practice. This is bound to happen, because the actual feelings of the various peoples and groups within the Church differ enormously. Some will take some particular expression of opinion as a matter of course, while others will regard it as a tactless criticism, utterly lacking in respect, of Church ordinances and customs. Some will feel frustrated, fearing that pronouncements and explanations always get put off until it is almost too late for them to be of any use. They will feel that a thing is only allowed when in fact it can no longer be stopped, when even the official representatives of the Church have become such children of their own age (but already almost out of date) that the thing they finally sanction and approve is a *fait accompli*, whereas if it had been allowed earlier it would have been the sign of a really liberating and redeeming attitude. Others will regard exactly the same thing as a destructive attack upon sanctified traditions which have established themselves through the wisdom of centuries and proved themselves by long practice to be sound and rich in blessings. Exactly the same sort of criticism may be in one case beneficial, or at least harmless, and in another have all the unfortunate consequences expected of it, encouraging an attitude of blasphemy and private rebellion. The position here is rather like that in different families: in one the children are allowed to criticize things openly and to express their own desires and complaints, and yet at the same time are most devoted and obedient children, whereas in another this freedom might undermine the parents' authority absolutely and in practice be a real threat to their ultimate right of decision. Obviously this depends on the way the children have been brought up. When they have been encouraged from their earliest days to voice their own desires and wishes quite frankly and yet at the same time have been brought up in a proper spirit of obedience, a frank exchange of views between them and their parents can do nothing but good and will never be regarded by either side as being impertinence or destructive criticism. But if they have been brought up to listen and obey, on the assumption that their parents' word is law; if, even when they are grown-up, they have to behave as though they could never have any views of their own; then any sudden permission to criticize will in fact undermine the authority of their parents. From this simple analogy—and it is no more, of course —it can be said, so far as our own problem here is concerned, that the people in the Church (young men in Holy Orders, the laity and so on) must be brought up in a responsible spirit of obedience and be able to make proper use of their right to express their opinions. They must learn

that this right to express their own views and to
criticize others does not mean licence to indulge
in savage attacks and arrogant presumption.
They must be brought up in a proper critical
spirit towards Church matters, not finding it
necessary to rave about anything that happens to
be in favour in the Church at the moment as
though it were the ultimate end of wisdom, and
yet able to unite this frame of mind with a
humble and at the same time dignified habit of
obedience. They must learn to unite the inevitable detachment of a critical public attitude with
a genuine and inspired love of the Church and
a genuine subordination and submission to the
actual official representatives of the Church.
They must learn that even in the Church there
can be a body something like Her Majesty's
Opposition, which in the course of Church history has always had its own kind of saints in its
ranks—the ranks of a genuine, divinely-willed
opposition to all that is merely human in the
Church and her official representatives.

They must learn—and this is not just a matter
of course, but means a serious effort of education
—that there are circumstances in which people
can have a real duty to speak their minds within
the permitted limits and in a proper spirit of
respect, even though this will not bring them
praise and gratitude "from above" (how many
examples there are of this in the history of the
saints!). They must also learn that it can be
God's will for them to live for a time, as New-
man said, "under a cloud", because they repre-
sent a spirit out of the ordinary which comes

23

from the Holy Spirit. They must learn to unite all this with a frank, simple, natural and utterly unlegalistic spirit of obedience and a ready good-will towards the Church's official representatives. Ultimately no formal rule can be laid down as to how to achieve a concrete synthesis of what are apparently such opposing virtues. It will come about only when people truly seek, not their own will and opinions and self-justification, but the will of God and the Church—ultimately, in fact, when people are saints. We live in a time of transition, which means, so far as our present question is concerned, at a time when certain outward forms which have so far been useful or at least have existed for a long time are now proving themselves less useful and effective in promoting Church authority. Therefore a somewhat greater range of expression of public opinion is allowable, assuming that the spiritual attitude of Catholics is such that it can bear this greater freedom without detriment to their spirit of obedience. Apart from anything else, the Church today should be more careful than ever before not to give even the slightest impression that she is of the same order as those totalitarian states for whom outward power and sterile, silent obedience are everything and love and free-dom nothing, and that her methods of government are those of the totalitarian systems in which public opinion has become a Ministry of Propaganda. But we—both those of us who are in authority and those who are under authority —are perhaps still accustomed here and there to certain patriarchal forms of leadership and

obedience which have no essential or lasting connection with the real stuff of Church authority
and obedience. When this is so, Church authorities may see even a justifiable expression of frank
opinion about Church matters as camouflaged
rebellion, or resentment against the Church Hierarchy. Even those not in authority may dislike
such free expression, because they are accustomed
to the old traditional ways.

In such transitional periods there are many
questions of a practical kind which will need a
long time for their solution, and the really contemporary ways in which public opinion is to
manifest itself within the Church are still to be
found. Patience is necessary on both sides. The
Church authorities must be patient, not regard-
ing every frank expression of opinion or criticism
as an attack upon themselves or on essential
Church principles and institutions, or as an
attempt to outvote them and their decisions.
Those under their authority must be patient, not
giving the impression that they regard every ad-
monition from above as an out-and-out attack
upon free expression within the Church or as an
absolute denial of the right of public opinion to
exist within the Church.

What conclusions may now be drawn from
what has been said, with particular regard to the
matter of the layman's actual behaviour within
the Church?

In the first place, the layman still has in this
respect a duty—an old duty, but always needing
to be re-emphasized—to educate himself in religious and theological matters up to a decent

level, corresponding to his intellectual level in other fields. He has his own kind of responsibility for the Church as a whole and for her concrete activity in the world of time. He is called upon to play his part and live up to his responsibilities in helping to create a state of public opinion within the Church. He is not just there to be given orders and to act as a silent, obedient servant. He can only do his duty as a member of the Church, thinking and working hand in hand with all the others and so sharing in the Church's public life, if he really knows something. He must know what his Church teaches. He must have a deep-rooted knowledge of where the fixed boundaries of his faith lie. He must not be left open to the sort of ideas and aspirations that would never have entered his head had he had a better religious education and a deeper knowledge of the Church's teaching. He must know something about Church history, so that he is not always ready to accept the latest thing, his own period's *dernier cri*, as the end of all wisdom. He must, within certain limits, know a very great deal. To begin with, he must have a really clear understanding of the Church's official teaching about all those matters which, because of his position in life and his personal relationships with others, concern him most intimately. Lacking this, he will be in danger of imagining that he can further his own interests and his own personal convictions only by adopting—unreflectively, and therefore all the more potently and dangerously—a kind of "double-think", acting towards heresies "cryptogamically", whilst at the same time keeping in line officially with the Church and theoretically acknowledging all her teaching. When a person does not know precisely what the Church teaches and does not teach, or to what degree any given item of her teaching is binding, then, even though he may want to be a true member of the Church for thoroughly worthy and indeed objectively valid reasons, he will be in danger of taking any actual or probable decision by the Church and "adopting it and turning it into a legal enactment", instead of understanding it from within and making it part and parcel of his very being. He will, moreover, run another risk: instead of being the spokesman of a genuine public opinion and a general attitude within the Church, he may find himself involved in a type of opinion and attitude that is far from public; that has in fact a subterranean element of heresy, including a camouflaged resentment against the "Roman system"—as people with that kind of mentality like to call the true Church.

Catholics who want to take a real share in the development of a public opinion within the Church must live like true Christians and make the Church's cardinal mysteries the basis of their personal life. There will naturally be room for differences of opinion on all the questions open to general discussion within the Church. If there is, as there should be, a real public opinion within the Church, not merely an unthinking reflection of the Church's official views, a certain tension is likely to exist around all those matters that are subject to change and hence to free

2 + 27

discussion. Unless we incorporate the Church's central truths and mysteries into our own living and see that the Church is most genuinely herself when she is proclaiming the Gospel's good tidings about the grace of God and administering the Christian sacraments, we shall tend, when we see signs of this tension, to overestimate its significance. The Church as a historical phenomenon will set our teeth on edge—and this will be entirely our own fault: and we shall partly, if not wholly, lose our inward joy in the Church and in the true life within her. Yet our Lord is alive in the Church; through her we can receive his body and hear words of true forgiveness— these and many other facts of a like kind are a thousand times more important than for instance the question as to whether the liturgy of Holy Saturday should be celebrated in the morning or the evening, whether the Church shows herself progressive enough in word and deed over some minor social question, whether the latest pastoral letter strikes one as being sound and modern or antiquated and creaking at the joints. It is only possible to combine this right sense of proportion about Church matters with the ability to share, calmly and constructively, in the development of a public opinion within the Church—and this without any resentment or bitterness or any indulgence in backbiting—if one is really in touch with the vital sources at the heart of the Church's supernatural activity.

Assuming that he fulfils these conditions, the layman must do all he can to make his own personal contribution to the development of a public opinion within the Church, and its dissemination outside her. Anyone who fails to do this is laying himself open, and rightly, to criticism. One cannot limit one's share in the life of the Church to going to Mass and receiving the sacraments and then go on to criticize everything the Church says and does, especially about ordinary social life. The layman should know his parish priest. He should also know (and this does not mean he must become a "joiner") that there are certain types of Church organization to which he is quite rightly expected to belong. There is such a thing as the Catholic Press, for instance. Now it seems doubtful whether this is always as good as it might be, but it will certainly never be any better than it is as long as people, educated Catholics in particular, simply assume that it is beneath their dignity to read it and support it. If people have any complaints about the Catholic Press, they should make them known to the people who can do something about it. And when the educated Catholic buys Catholic books, and buys the right kind of Catholic books, he is partaking to some extent in a sort of general vote about them, helping in the organization and management of the Catholic book trade and at the same time promoting the right kinds of books and getting rid of pious trash. Writing to newspapers, magazines and book publishers is perhaps not a Continental habit, but this does not necessarily mean that it is a foolish one or just a kind of game. Assuming that the people who do it are sensible and that it is not simply a method of killing time, writing to papers can be quite a good way of getting some sort of public opinion going. Again, how many educated Catholics have ever written their bishop a letter about a question that is worrying them? Probably very few. Is this because they have no confidence in their bishop, or do they regard the Hierarchy as a sort of heavenly body from which the most that can be expected is an occasional pastoral letter to which it would be presumptuous to answer a word of thanks or concern or objection? Such a response would assuredly be most gratefully received. The part played by the laity in parish life, in the parish's economic affairs, Church schools and such like, is far greater in the Anglo-Saxon countries than it is in some parts of the Continent. Must this always be so? There was a time when Catholic congresses and other customs of a like kind, whereby the Church spoke out in public, outside the range of the pulpit, were organized by Catholic laypeople with far more spontaneous enthusiasm for the Kingdom of God than they are today. Couldn't this state of affairs be restored? Must these undertakings always give us the impression of being simply an unavoidable dreary routine? Some time ago a prominent layman complained in an Austrian magazine that the laity had not been consulted about the arrangements for the yearly mission. Whether this was so or not is not the point. If the laity could only make their views known (and they would, when asked), it would undoubtedly be very useful before such large-scale ventures took place. And why shouldn't the clergy make this a way of finding out the kind of question the laity regard as particularly urgent and want to hear discussed from the pulpit? Are there any Church organizations, or at any rate societies with some sort of Catholic basis, that dare, or even think, to pass on their worries and wishes and their queries about the part the Church is playing in public life by way of suggestions to the powers-that-be in the Church? One hopes that there are, but does this kind of thing happen often? In the secular sphere there are bodies that go in for market inquiries, Gallup polls and such like, and though it is true that salvation is not a matter of statistics, certainly not so far as the Catholic Church is concerned, nevertheless similar investigations in the religious field might easily be very useful. But if questionnaires of a rather more subtle kind, involving more than merely a count of heads in different parishes, are to lead to anything, ordinary Catholics, Catholics who know what life is and what the real conditions of life are today, will have to learn to say what they think. Recently an Austrian religious magazine made an inquiry of this kind into the question how many people were making use of what is known nowadays as "marriage guidance". Such results could be quite useful for priests. How many Catholics write to Catholic papers? The number is still far too small. Not that ordinary Catholics can be expected to know their theology better than priests; nor are priests quite so hidebound as many Catholics seem to think; furthermore, ordinary Catholics should only speak about these fundamental things when they have really studied the question and have something to say. Nevertheless the fact remains that questions of faith, questions in which the Church and religion are involved, are not esoteric matters in the face of which laymen must be seen and not heard. They should be expected to join in too. But precisely for this reason they must do it properly, off their own bat. These are just a few of the ways of helping to foster the growth of a public opinion within the Church, and others can easily be imagined: they will all provide an opportunity for the ordinary Catholic to fulfil a personal duty, the duty of taking his own part in the Church's life and missionary work.

There is one other point that may be mentioned, to bring these reflections to an end. In the course of the Church's history there have, at different times, been a number of different ways in which public opinion has been able to make itself felt within the Church. It exerted some sort of influence on the conduct of the Hierarchy through such things as the share taken by the laity in the election of bishops and in nominating the rest of the clergy, in admitting people to baptism and reconciling repentant sinners; the right of patronage; the rights of medieval and modern governments with regard to the filling of bishoprics; and so on. But compared with the present-day expressions of public opinion these old forms had one outstanding feature: they were properly drawn up from the legal point of view and formed part of the layman's rights within the Church. They were of their time, of course, and were often bound up with irregularities: no one would wish them back again exactly as they were; nevertheless, it is true to say that there is by comparison very little, if any, recognized way in which public opinion can make itself felt within the Church today, according to modern canon law. This does not mean that there is no such thing as a public opinion within the Church. It would be quite wrong to say that. But it would not be wrong to say that there are hardly any ways with the force of law behind them whereby public opinion can operate within the Church. Whether this is a pity or not is another question, which need not necessarily be answered in the affirmative here. But at least the problem can be stated. Today, we know, is the day of Catholic Action, when ordinary Catholics are supposed to be sharing, to some extent, the Church's duties and responsibilities with the official Hierarchy. Now, if this is not to remain simply a matter of theory, an "ideal", but to become the fullest possible reality, it would seem to require—as also in the long run it would effect—the growth of new, legally recognized ways, which today hardly exist, if they exist at all, in which the laity could co-operate with the clergy. The fact that these rights do not at present exist within the Church, either by *jus divinum* or as a *jus humanum*, is no reason why they should not do so again in the future. They must always of course remain within and dependent upon the *jus divinum* of the Hierarchy and what is to a certain extent the Hierarchy's exclusive power of leadership, granted it by our Lord himself; nevertheless there are still such things as layman's rights. The granting of such rights may be a benefit all round, in fact at certain times and in certain conditions it may be an obligation on the Church. How these rights, whether of a general or a particular kind, would look in practice, is a subject that naturally cannot be gone into here. The question here is simply whether the influence of public opinion within the Church, as something which exists and should exist, might not in certain respects, in some form or other, be given some sort of legal backing so as to become effective and effective in the right way.

Ultimately it all boils down to the fact that every individual Christian is responsible in his own day and way for the Church and the life of the Church. If the reader has become a little more aware of his responsibility in this respect as a result of what has been said, then I have achieved what I set out to do. St. Cyprian, writing in the middle of the third century, began a treatise on patience by observing that he had to assume in his reader the existence of the thing he was about to recommend. This present essay may end on a similar note. Many things that have been said in the course of it are probably highly debatable and in need of more profound treatment than they have been accorded here. To expect them to be read and pondered with a good will was to assume the existence of that which in fact they are concerned with, namely, the belief that there is and should be something in the nature of free speech within the Church as there

34

is outside it, and that consequently even people who have nothing more to offer than their own private and personal opinions have a right to express these and to be given a favourable hearing when they do so.

THE PROSPECT FOR CHRISTIANITY

I

The Christian must "profess" his faith. This
faith of his includes, amongst other things, the
knowledge that it is "glad tidings" from God to
every succeeding age of men, suited to every con
dition, easily recognizable as being of divine
origin. He must know that the gates of hell will
never prevail against the Church; that Christianity provides the solution to every problem.
But the Christian of today, anxious to live his
faith and to bear his own personal witness to it,
often finds it hard to see his faith as suited to his
own age, to remember that it is indeed glad
tidings from God, safe from the onslaughts of
any hostile power. What is he to do: give up his
belief in the triumphant power of Christianity
as a faith for the future, or put himself in
blinkers and try to ignore the sober realities of
the age he lives in? Usually he does neither: he
is a Christian, but a half-hearted one; he is half-
hearted, but won't admit it, because as a Christian he is afraid to. This is all the more dan-
gerous in that every Christian is not only the
object of the Church's spiritual care as someone
destined for salvation but at the same time a
member of the Church and as such partly
responsible for her continued existence and the
fulfilment of her mission in the world. Every
Christian has to some extent or other, according

to his condition in life, the duties and responsibilities of a missionary and an apostle, and it is therefore a matter of some importance whether he acquits himself of these cheerfully or in a state of fear. And it must be said that when in fact, shedding our illusions, we come to inquire about the "mood" of the average Christian today, we find it difficult to reach any particularly cheering conclusions in the matter, either about the clergy or about the laity.

Frank confession harms no one. If there is anything humiliating in it, it is not the actual confessing but the thing we have to confess, which is still with us even if we do not admit it, but go around in a dejected half-hearted frame of mind trying to keep the dreadful truth from others and ourselves. Let us admit quite frankly what the position is. We are the people who feel out of place in the world. We are the frustrated ones, preferring to bear witness to our faith (in fear and trembling, but before the world, not before God) where it suits us, rather than where it might not go down so well. We do not feel highly optimistic about things. We often have the feeling—naturally without admitting it to ourselves —that we are talking into the empty air. When we speak about our Christianity, the most precious thing we possess, we are received—or so it seems anyway—by deaf ears and hearts closed against us, rather than with the eager attention of minds thoroughly alert. We often feel as though we cannot hope to speak to most people in any way that they could understand. We have, too, an unpleasant sense, whenever we hear the sound of our own voice, that it is not particularly surprising that nobody listens to us. Doesn't a great deal of what we say sound strange in our own ears—outmoded, utterly out of date? It is still lodged in our heads, as a hangover from the days when we learned our catechism, but it no longer comes from our hearts: so it is hardly to be wondered at that it no longer gets into the heads of other people.

If anyone begins to protest at this point that he himself is a thoroughly convinced Christian, he had better be careful. For he might get asked the question whether his own actual words and behaviour are as attractive and compelling to others as they should be, if his claim to be full of courageous orthodoxy is to ring true. If he lays the blame on the evil times he lives in, and the hard, guilty hearts of the people he has failed to win over to his own faith, then he must be prepared to answer the further question as to whether, and how, he can be so sure that his fellow men—whom as a Christian he is supposed not to judge—are as wickedly hard-hearted as he says they are and whether it wouldn't be more Christian—because more humble—to blame himself instead of them? He must answer the question as to whether the times really are as evil as he makes them out to be, or whether it may not be that we ourselves have not grown up sufficiently to cope with our own day as well as earlier generations of Christians did with theirs, when in fact things were no worse, but only different.

We are often quite intimidated, quite sullen

38

and bitter—almost embittered—and frustrated, quite content if the rest of the world is merely prepared to tolerate us. Of course we are furious if anyone actually says this to our face. We don't want to be like this—and that is quite right of us. We don't want to be taken for the kind of people who have tamely succumbed to circumstance. We are not cowards or deserters; if we were, how could we be servants of Jesus Christ? The will of our faith, our spirit, speaks out clearly: we will to be other than in fact we are, human beings whose many-levelled nature has not, or not yet, or not completely, been mastered by the grace of Christ. But that is what we are. And any improvement can only come from a frank confession of this—a confession that has nothing to do with compromise.

But this is not all. We must go on to confess that not only are we half-hearted, but that we believe—unconsciously—that we have every reason to be half-hearted, to be in the apostolic dumps. Let us leave aside for the moment the fact of our own mediocrity, the fact that our minds, our characters, our lives with all their anxieties, seem to put the light of the Gospel in the shade and sometimes almost under a bushel. Apart from all this, we seem to ourselves to have enough objective grounds outside ourselves to account for our own private spirit of defeatism; and because these grounds seem to be facts, firm hard facts which in our short, circumscribed lives there seems no possibility of changing, we feel we have no hope of ever damming up the sources of our creeping dejection, which threatens, like some illness, to go with us to the grave.

Let us take a good look round. After the two thousand years of its history Catholic Christianity is still confined to a small fraction of the human race, and, despite all successes in the mission field, this minority is growing steadily smaller, because numerically the human race is increasing more rapidly than the number of conversions.

In vast areas of the world Christianity is a persecuted religion, slowly but surely being throttled out of existence by all the means available to modern states, with their police forces and their systems of thought control now beginning to penetrate into the ultimate recesses of the human heart and brain. And even if we take the most optimistic view we can of the underground movements and modern catacomb Churches in these areas of the world and in fact accept all that is said about them in Church papers and missionary magazines, this can do nothing to lessen our alarm. If things go on in the same way for a few more decades—and where is any change likely to come from?—Christianity (and that means primarily Catholic Christianity) will be reduced in our half of the world to something like what the Hussites once were, or the Waldensians, or the Dutch Jansenists in the nineteenth century: it may continue to exist, but so far as the world and world history generally are concerned it won't count—though the Church is supposed to stand out as a "sign lifted up among the nations". From the human and purely secular point of view it will have no future whatsoever.

And what about the position on the other side of the Iron Curtain, where some of us live, still live? A civilization, or rather a lack of civilization, characterized by the mass-man and technology, by noise and pleasure, worry and anxiety, the atrophy of the religious sense, by utter sexual licence and the disintegration of the instincts: by manufacture rather than creation, the artificial instead of the God-given; by the flight from self, the profane and the profaned; a world from which God is utterly absent. The Christian religion and its adherents seem to be still there only because the old order is taking so long to vanish completely. And a horrible dilemma rears its head; for when Christianity tries to adapt modern methods—yesterday's methods, tomorrow's methods—to its own purposes, it seems to become just as artificial, just as manufactured, just as fiercely organized, as everything else; and if it ignores the new methods it seems to lag hopelessly behind the times.

If we look a little nearer home, we seem to be faced with the same depressing state of affairs. Germany is once more a missionary land, or it should be, i.e., it needs to be brought back to the Church. Anyone who does not adopt the tactics of the ostrich, or who does not simply concentrate on the fact that he is one of the few Christians left, can feel it every day. We live in a pagan country with a Christian past. We live among the remains of Christianity. But it can no longer be said that from the point of view of this world alone, the dominant tendency of our time, the major impulse behind present-day events, is taking our history towards Christianity. We Christians are on the defensive. All that we do seems at best only to delay a process set firmly against us, never to reverse its direction. Every attempt we make to take up the offensive seems to come to an end before it has really got going. In fact we often defend historical façades, the laws and customs of what was once socially, politically and intellectually a Christian community, with the secret feeling that we have no right to be doing so because the surface of our community is really more Christian than the reality behind it, and because we, as citizens, seem at the moment to possess more in the way of social and political rights than the number of really convinced Christians amongst us warrants. Moreover, so long as the private individual is allowed to go on living the new paganism in his own way this often seems to be to a surprising extent far more tolerant towards the Christian externals of public life than were the furious secularists and anti-clericals of the nineteenth century. Have people become kinder and more tolerant towards us in these pagan times because they are not so afraid of us as they used to be, because fundamentally they feel that they no longer need take us seriously? However that may be, on this particular point we must not be in too much of a hurry to take comfort from the kindnesses, little or great, that the great world of unbelievers is prepared to show towards Christianity today, to the Church and the Pope and our bishops, as though the position were quite different from what it was, for instance, in the last century. The spring-times of Catholic and Christian awakening that followed the two world wars have gone for ever and entirely. To change the metaphor, that period looks now, in retrospect, like the advance of a deep river flowing irresistibly along, which seems for a moment to turn back on itself because something or other has blocked its path. We have become strangers to the world; the world itself seems to be calling the tune, and to regard Christianity as something left over from the boasted past of the West, something fit only to be embalmed in some museum or to serve the dreams of childish romantics and the improvement schemes of political restorationists.

And this Church of ours in tired old Europe, this Church that is us, seems to be tired herself. The Faith now seems in many respects to be just marking time theoretically and to be no longer lived existentially, just as so many people go on saying what a wonderful musician Bach is and yet listen to nothing but jazz on the wireless. Where can you hear a sermon on hell these days? How many people, when they see someone faced with everlasting damnation, cry out in a loud voice, with conviction, in anguish, "Save your soul!"? How many still have, deep in their hearts, the Christian fear of death and the Last Judgement? How many are capable of feeling desperately worried—I mean in the quiet of their own minds, not as an official gesture—when some Catholic acquaintance of theirs dies without the last sacraments? How many, as shamelessly

thick-skinned as the saints, dare to whisper in
the ear of those who don't want to listen that
they must be converted and have pity on themselves? How many priests are there who go off
and face the Areopagites of the secular world as
St. Paul did? How many people have these priests
converted, not by seeing them by appointment
but by going out to find them like missionaries
—and by going a long way, even if only over the
seas and abysses of the mind that exist today? It
is strange: when the modern priest makes a missionary onslaught on anybody, he usually does
it by reminding the person concerned that he is
really a Christian already (i.e., baptized and
brought up as a Catholic). Why doesn't he do it
instead with the thought that this man is a pagan
who must become a Christian? Today we treat
even pagans as though they belonged to some
Christian denomination, as do Protestants.

And what about Christian doctrine itself, as
it is to be found in the inner sanctums of the
Church? Isn't Christian theology a tame thing
today, so far as we Catholics are concerned, anyway? An awful lot of it is being produced, but
it is alarmingly little compared with all the other
books being produced about the intellectual—
and unintellectual—life of the times. Theological "modernism" was, on the whole, rightly cen-
sured and condemned to silence; but at the same
time the safe and trusty theologians hardly give
the impression that they have the power to
preach the old faith to a new age in a new, fresh
way. And isn't there something rather strange
and disturbing about the way the emphasis seems

44

to shift about, from one Christian truth to another? A Christian social movement is highly thought of, but is that the most important thing, in the light of the Gospels?

Furthermore, are there not what might be called "cryptogam" heresies, which cannot be detected because they are not theoretically formulated, but only practically lived, heresies which never make any actual protest but simply let the Church have her say and then do the opposite and whisper it in private conversation—heresies in behaviour, in attitude to life, in actual living, which can go hand in hand quite ingenuously, or ingeniously, with Church membership?

And then there is the matter of the holiness of our own lives. Leaving aside all the scandals —and there have been quite a few—we have only to make a few inquiries into the general spiritual and ascetic level of the lives of average people like ourselves, into the figures for the priesthood and the monastic orders; we have only to look round about us for examples of the "inspired folly" of the saints—why, we don't even know today, as former generations did, what such folly would look like! —and the answer is quite plain.

In short, we have, it seems, every objective reason to be resigned and defeatist in our attitude. Does not all this suggest, or rather demand, that we should adopt a sober realism and see things as they actually are? What is one to say in answer to this?

Let me try now to put all that has been said above into a nutshell, into a brief and somewhat more precise theological formula, at the risk of

oversimplifying the matter and of dodging a few
answers to individual questions. We Christians,
then, against our own deepest will, are often
fainthearted in our approach to our apostolic
duties because, when we look out upon the present state of Christianity and the Church in our
own country and the world, we seem to see no
prospect that our struggle to get official Catholic
Christianity recognized and accepted in the tangible reality of the world and our own history
(even to the extent already reached in the West)
will end in anything but failure. Look closely at
what I have said. I do not say that we are afraid
that Christianity will disappear off the face of
the earth. That, from the religious point of view,
would be a heresy and the end of all faith—if it
were presented as being in any sense a justification for such a fear. The fear itself would be a
sign of cowardice, which, as believers, we should
have to fight hard against and disavow. Moreover, even on a purely secular view of history,
on an estimation of the position based wholly on
this world, it would be childishly short-sighted.
No world-wide phenomenon as vast, both
materially and spiritually, as Christianity, as
deep, as strongly-rooted in every sphere of life
and culture, could, even on the most pessimistic
estimates, be in danger of disappearing off the
face of the earth in any foreseeable future. This
is certain, quite apart from God's grace and
power, and his everlasting promises. Such a danger does not exist, even in the case of the other
great world religions like Mohammedanism and
Buddhism. It is still more inconceivable in the

case of Christianity. For Christianity—and this can never be undone—has been, historically, the religion behind the one civilization whose intellectual, cultural, political and religious activity and expansion has created world history as we now know it, the interpenetration of the histories of all the different races into one, for the first time since the dispersal of the nations related in Genesis. Such a religion would not disappear entirely from the face of the earth in any foreseeable future even if it were not a thing created and preserved by the living God, the Lord of the Ages. The question that tempts us to be defeatist (and it needs to be frankly stated) is, rather, simply this: now that human history has become one, will Christianity go on being a force in the international field, to at least the same degree as it has been so far in Western civilization and the European society of nations? This is not simply a question of fact which we can leave to the future, as having no religious or theological importance. For we cannot simply say that as long as Christianity goes on existing to the end of time, in the persons of a few representatives left over as a sort of atavistic remnant from the past, then God's promise that the gates of hell shall not prevail against it has been fulfilled. Nor can we simply say that the Church came into being through a few (from a purely worldly point of view) hopelessly misguided people who believed in the bodily resurrection of an idealist who had been hanged on the gallows, and yet that she was, even at that stage, actually the Church, with all her essential concomitants, and that therefore

47

she can again be reduced to the same embryonic stage without there being any reason for disquiet on religious or theological grounds. For this is precisely the question. Can such a retrogression take place in the case of something that has, from the historical point of view, set out on an essentially one-way track, without this being a sign that the thing in question is in imminent danger of collapse? Will it not seem to everyone to be destined for extinction, even though historical remnants of it still go on existing for what seems for ever? And will not those watching this retrogression feel compelled to say that this Church was not founded by God with the promise that it would triumph over death? Again, *vice versa*: from the theological point of view the Church is not always equally herself, irrespective of whether she is a scared little group or a great society covering the whole world. The fact that she began as a tiny flock does nothing to controvert this. A human being, too, begins in a very embryonic and helpless way, and yet he realizes his full being as planned and intended only when he is fully grown. The Church is not merely a large or a small number of people, as chance may see fit to decide; she is a "sign lifted up amongst the nations", and she must bear the sign of her divine foundation plainly for all men of goodwill to see. Her vitality, her holiness, her inexhaustible fecundity, must be plain to all eyes in the open forum of the wide world and in the history and civilization of the world; thus she herself will be a motive of faith. Could she be such—the question is at least worth asking—if her real position in the history of the peoples of the world were gradually to decline? This question, even in the restricted form in which we have phrased it, is not easy to answer at first sight.

When we try to explain what has been said above and to go beyond the merely factual element in it—our half-heartedness and the obvious reasons for such an attitude—and try to discover how we can put an end to it, we find ourselves faced with two problems. We have to ask ourselves, firstly, whether the actual fact of Christianity's being on the defensive (assuming we simply accept this "factual condition" as a fact) is a good and sufficient reason for our unacknowledged half-heartedness. Then we have to turn to the actual fact itself and ask ourselves how we must understand it. The first question, therefore, is concerned with our anxiety, the second with the reason for our anxiety. And the first question comes first because (however strange this may seem at first sight) ultimately, from the theological point of view, the answer to it is quite independent of the answer to the second question, which is predominantly taken from the philosophy of history.

II

Let us assume to begin with that all the grounds mentioned above for our apostolical defeatism are good and sufficient ones. Has our defeatism, then, a right to exist, just because we know that there is a real cause behind it? The answer is—even on this (problematical) assumption—no. Why not?

From the point of view of the Catholic faith a defeatist attitude towards Christianity is not in any way justifiable on the above "grounds". For faith consists precisely in hoping against hope, in holding firmly to something beyond human reason as the ground of all existence. Faith means walking on water, standing up straight when there is every reason to fall down. Faith means including God in one's scheme of things, though God himself remains outside all human power and beyond any possible scheme which human beings may fabricate; it means building on grace, which is always and only grace, i.e., an event undeserved, always purely actual, depending entirely on God's gracious will. If we are Christians we are called upon to put all our trust in God, in God alone, without working out in advance whether our faith has any chance or not. "Has Christianity still got a chance?" is a question that as Christians—assuming we are such to begin with—we cannot ask. The moment we do so in earnest, then, to that extent, we have already left the ground of faith. We are demanding, not God or the grace of God, but some guarantee which we can hold in our hands, something sufficient and effective in itself, before we are prepared to believe and trust him. We are prepared to fight only if victory is in fact assured from the outset. We are prepared to say Yes to God, if we have first been allowed to say Yes to ourselves and our own situation. We are prepared to appear before God only as people

already justified, instead of surrendering ourselves to him as people needing justification. Our
whole modern attitude to faith simply takes concrete shape in the question that faces us; it is not
especially strange. For faith, without God's
elevating and healing grace, is always the Impossible. It is of course true that there exist
grounds for faith which are in themselves objective and demonstrable, which the believer can
see for himself and explain to others; true, too,
that the grace of faith is offered to everyone, so
that there is always a real possibility of discussion
about the Faith, even with people who do not as
yet share it. Nevertheless, in actual concrete fact,
faith only comes through the grace of God, and
this alone can provide the concrete individual
human being—wounded in mind and will as he
is through original sin—with the assistance he
needs if he is to go beyond all those other
"grounds" that seem to him to justify his un-
belief. But if the grace of God is necessary, and
yet at the same time quite different from the
rational, objectively verifiable motives for faith
springing purely from this world, then, if one
leaves the grace of faith out of account, it must
always seem in actual concrete fact as though it
were more sensible and prudent not to believe
than to believe, as though there were always
grounds that seemed to justify the wisdom of the
world. But whatever is valid and durable for all
time is (along with other things) especially rele-
vant to our own question here: the fact is that
we only really begin to believe when we do not
start by asking whether Christianity has any

chance today. If the specifying inner motive of our faith is judged wholly by this world's standards—which means, in the present case, the empirically ascertainable prospects of success, again judged by standards of the world, for the Church and Christianity—then our faith is a human achievement, brittle, destined to be surpassed and renounced like all human things, and not an act of God upon us, accepted by a free act of will. And so, *vice versa*, if faith is an act of God upon us, something that takes place by the power of God, then it cannot depend on whether there is any predetermined certainty that the chances of Christianity are good, leaving God's word and promise out of account as things never adequately realized in the "facts" of this world.

The question of our private defeatist attitude thus turns out to be a brutally simple question about faith itself, the question of whether we really believe. If we do, then what follows from the facts we put forward as grounds for our concealed anxiety is, even though they *are* facts, precisely nothing. We may not know *how* we are going to pull through, but we must believe that we shall, and this not *in spite of* the fact that, to our great surprise, we do not know how, but *because* our very faith consists precisely in expecting not to know how in advance, and having to build on God's word alone—his word having more weight and validity for us than any number of alarming "facts" that may come into our ken. These facts, rightly considered—i.e., from a believer's point of view—force us to decide either

52

to believe as faith itself would have us believe, or to be unbelievers; what they do not do is to force us into a defeatist condition of half-belief that goes on fighting without really believing in ultimate success. We are asked to decide whether or not we are the kind of people who know from their faith that in human impotence is manifested the power of God—and it alone, and in utter ignorance of how this will come about; whether or not we value the darkness of the world more highly than the light of God, the fleeting show of history above God's patience and long-suffering; whether or not we regard the folly of the Cross as something wiser than the wisdom of the world and that out-of-date thing called Christianity as a thing more modern than the "modern world". The "unpropitious" facts are not an obstacle or a source of surprise and disenchantment to people who really believe; they are to be expected: it is just a question of girding up one's loins and facing them boldly, under the inspiration and protection of the Faith.

Does this mean that all believers who are trying wholeheartedly to do God's will are quite free from the kind of anxiety that has been described above? Have they so completely conquered it that not the faintest trace remains? Are we expected to behave as though it were not in fact within the very marrow of our bones? Are we supposed to regard it as at best a fairly obvious symptom of the weakness of our faith? These questions are not easy to answer. We must certainly make a decent effort to be happy and enthusiastic about our faith, to be free from anxiety and imbued with a determined optimism, to have a thoroughly convinced faith, in fact; if we fail to do this with every power at our command we are really "tempting" God. But faith can be real faith, triumphant, utterly devoted, and yet manifest itself in continual struggle too. Ultimately it is not we but only God who can decide in which of these two ways his grace will choose to manifest itself to us. It may be that today more than in any other age the grace will be granted us—and a real grace it is!—to be strong in spite of our feeling of helplessness, full of hope in spite of our dismay, sure of ultimate victory though sorely besieged. Why should not Christians, nailed to the cross of their historical situation, have to cry out as our Lord himself cried out, "My God, my God, why hast thou forsaken me?" Why should they not have to share their Redeemer's bitter agony, sweating blood as they too lie prostrate on the ground? The more, therefore, that we have to fight exhaustion and cowardice and unacknowledged faintheartedness in ourselves and denounce these things in others, the more we should calmly confess (thereby giving God's grace its proper due), "Yes, we are those who so often hardly know which way to turn, who frequently do not know the right answers, who only have enough spiritual bread in our baskets for one day at a time and have to hope to build our future on that, having no idea where tomorrow's bread is to come from, except that it will come from God." The world has to bluster its way through, turning all its communiqués into proclamations of everlasting victory. The Christian has no need of this. His *Credo* includes those few words spoken down from the Cross, and the pages of Church history have therefore no need to be a collection of victorious proclamations. "In the world you will have sorrow", we have been told by him who is Lord of History, so why shouldn't we allow ourselves to admit it: "Yes, we have sorrow"? To the believer, who is always conscious of a further dimension of existence far beyond this world, "things are going badly for us" means not that things are going badly for *us*, but that things are going badly for God and God's cause; whereas, so far as "things are going well" is concerned, in the logic of faith in which God is included (and faith alone can do this) this saying is perfectly compatible with the first.

III

Once this position has been accepted, i.e., that the Faith is something that can judge everything but never be judged itself, then, and only then, can we go on and take a sober look at the apparent "facts" that cause all of us so much anxiety and distress and constitute a permanent temptation to defeatism so far as the Faith is concerned. How are these facts in fact to be understood? One can do one's best to present apparently objective facts, and yet really be giving an interpretation with a strong subjective bias instead of making an objective statement. One can seem to be merely repeating something, and yet in fact be saying something quite different. Two eyewitnesses of a raging battle may say for instance, "There's a retreat going on", and to the more short-sighted one this may mean the admission of an annihilating defeat, whilst to the other, with the longer view, it can signify a piece of strategy promising eventual victory. So making a list of the reasons for our defeatism, as we did at the beginning of this essay, is by no means the end of the matter. We still have to ask what these reasons are really saying—what, looked at more closely, they mean. In attempting to answer this, many of the philosophical and theological points known to us from our history must inevitably be left unanswered, of course, but even so some consideration of this problem cannot be entirely fruitless, for it will at least show us that we need to adopt a very critical attitude towards our immediate uncorroborated first impressions, and that a great deal that is included under the heading of our "facts" is really tinged with subjectivism from the outset.

It has been pointed out already that from the purely theological point of view it is unsatisfactory that there should be a mere handful of Christians in existence, and that the Church, once having "grown up", needs to continue as a great force in the world and world history. And precisely because it is a source of anxiety to us not to know whether the Church can go on being this, and if so how, that some attempt to see the matter in the light of the theology of history will not be out of place here. It should then become clear that our alarm at the prospect of a much reduced Church has less reason behind it than might appear at first sight. I will say quite plainly then, that the kind of public, external importance which the Church has had for the last thousand or fifteen hundred years, and which we still instinctively regard as the obvious standard whereby to judge of the Church's achievement, was not only a concrete manifestation of what the Church must be and (once having attained it) must go on being in accordance with her supernatural essence and mission. It was also (though to what degree it is not easy to lay down) the result of a purely arbitrary and temporary concatenation of historical circumstances, so that if these pass away, there is possible a change in the Church's public significance without change in the Church's essence thereby being brought into question.

To explain and support this statement, the matter must be gone into a little more closely. Perhaps the practical consequences to be drawn from it will justify the extent to which I am obliged to go into detail. To begin with I shall offer an idea of a rather *a priori* theological kind, and then I shall approach the matter from a more historical-empirical point of view, and I shall try to show that neither from the *a priori* theological point of view nor from the *a posteriori* historical point of view could we expect the particular form in which the Church's prestige and "power" in public life has been handed down to us so far to continue unchanged in the future.

I start from the assumption that Christianity and the Church will go on being a stumbling-block and a point of contention until the end of time, and that this is not merely a fact for all to see. It is something more, part of a mysterious "destiny", stressed again and again in Scripture, whereby human guilt, something that should not be, remains everlastingly encompassed within the divine scheme of things. Not that God wills human guilt to exist; but he uses it throughout history, even though it is against his will, to help him to realize his plans. Thus in the eyes of the believer, who tries to see everything from God's own standpoint, this "inevitable" element is not simply something that he may take into account if he feels like it, but something that he is obliged to take into account, something that he has been expecting quite calmly all along and can never be surprised at. What form will this hostility to the Church—this everlasting hostility, which need never surprise us, which we must always look for—what form will it take in the future?

So long as the Church was in practice limited to one area of history and civilization, Western Europe, the "hostility" could come from "outside", because there was in fact an "outside", whilst at the same time the Church could be, so to speak, "omnipotent", the uncontested lord and master of this limited area, with all her opponents outside her—practical heresies ultimately deriving from the East and Christendom's traditional enemy, the Turk.

But one day this "outside" will cease to exist —and this may take centuries, of course—because the Church has become universal in the "outward" sense too; then (the other essential condition) the hitherto separate histories of the various nations of the world will have come together to form one single whole, in which each separate race, each historical situation, becomes of inner significance to all the others. When this at last takes place, the hostility to the Church, from the theology of history's point of view, can no longer come from "outside" but will be obliged—in the mysterious sense of destiny mentioned above—to arise within Christianity itself in the form of schism and apostasy; otherwise the Church would be either uncontested master or, to a certain extent, the insular Church of a particular civilization in decline. Neither of these alternatives is possible. As a matter of fact the first signs of the split and the de-Christianization of the Western world by the Reformation and Renaissance "enlightenment" came at the very moment when Europe was beginning to expand across the world and the Church was becoming a world Church in actual concrete fact. By spreading abroad among all the pagan nations she became a Church *amongst* the pagan nations. This dual event was accompanied of course by a vast amount of human wrongdoing and appalling tragedy, but nevertheless, seen from the bird's-eye view of a theology of history, it took place within the context of a mysterious destiny. To the Christian believer, this destiny can never be a matter for surprise or dismay: it is to be expected, for guilt and hostility to our Lord are indeed to be expected until the end of time. The loss of the Church's absolute power in public

life, which existed throughout the Middle Ages
—and we may regard the Middle Ages as having
come to an end with the French Revolution—
was thus, theologically speaking, to be expected,
although it involved so much incidental evil.
The medieval form of the Church's power over
society, the State, and civilization in general,
cannot by any means be regarded as something
essentially demanded by the nature of the
Church, if it is her destiny to be a permanent
stumbling-block and at the same time a truly
universal Church: that form was only possible as
long as the Church was the Church of a more
or less restricted area. The moment the West
became an unenclosed part of world-history, such
a form was impossible, for then hostility to the
Church had to exist either everywhere or no-
where. But because it had to exist, it had to exist
everywhere. "O you uncomprehending ones,
had not Christ to suffer?" applies here too, in
connection with our Lord's suffering in the history of the world.

As a matter of fact—and here we come to the
more empirical side of our consideration—even
the medieval form of the Church's position in
public life did not spring solely and entirely
from the supernatural power of Christianity and
the Church. In its actuality at least, if not in its
theological essence, it was also the result of a
concatenation of historical events that were time-
bound and of this world, a compound of history
and civilization rather than anything purely
theological. Every "medieval period", one might
say—i.e., every civilization that is based princi-

pally on a peasant population and small townships, and remains in a static condition over a long period of time—has its own uncontroverted dominant religion, no matter whether it is true or false, comes from above or below, or is known as medieval Mohammedanism or the feudal Shintoism of medieval Japan or anything else. The supernatural power of Christianity is not revealed by the mere fact that, like the dominant religions in other civilizations, it has exerted well-nigh uncontested absolute authority over human hearts and civilized institutions for a period of time that was bound one day to pass. This belief, beloved by so many people, will not really hold water for any historian or philosopher of history. The power of Christianity is to be found rather in the fact that on the disappearance of these passing temporal historical situations it has manifested, even on the empirical level, and despite all its apostasies and casualties, an incomparably greater power of resistance and persistence than any of the other religions which have had their own happy Middle Ages. And, further, in the fact that the Church's position in medieval Europe was such that Christianity was able to come forth in full strength from that civilization and accompany it throughout the world and thus become a universal religion on the empirical level too.

We thus undoubtedly have the right, indeed the duty, to face the fact squarely—and not simply give it a grudging acknowledgement— that the form in which the Church manifests itself in the life of society in general may change.

But despite the disturbing element in this fact—
namely the de-Christianization of the West—
there is still no excuse for timidity. How the new
manifestation of the Church's essential nature
will appear, in the general context of what is
now a unified world history, still remains to be
seen, and not much can be said about it at the
moment. The Church will still be the Church;
she will be present—as a concrete challenge to
all men at all times, which in the past was by
no means the case. She will appear more personal
and less institutional in nature, more on the side
of the individual's own personal initiative and
less dependent on the preventive power of established cultural factors such as customs, traditions,
laws and State regulations which exist indepen-
dently of the individual. Whether this kind of
Church authority is less powerful, so far as the
Church's fundamental supernatural mission is
concerned, than the old form it is destined to
supplant, is a question that can just as easily be
answered in the negative as in the affirmative. In
all that relates to our supernatural salvation, the
Church's power and authority in the world are
not obliged to be absolutely fixed and unvarying,
nor must the way she acts upon the world always
take the same form just because (as we believe)
she cannot undergo any essential change. What
we see today is in many respects not primarily a
decline of the Church's influence, so far as salvation is concerned, but a change in the way her
influence takes effect. It must be remembered
that the Church's existence as a public body and
her authority in the social and cultural life of

the day do not exist for their own sake but for the sake of the salvation of souls. These things can only have any meaning and justify their existence in so far as they serve this end. Anyone who has lived in what is superficially a rather churchy atmosphere will know that such an atmosphere does not necessarily help on the work of salvation. It may, for instance, be doubted whether the power of the Papacy in the days of the Church State did more for the salvation of souls than the Pope's influence at the present time on people living in the same area. And has the Church, so far as her supernatural effect on the salvation of souls is concerned, any more influence on the public life of Spain, despite her authority there, than she has in the United States? In short, we have a right to regard the apparent disappearance of the Church's public authority, as compared with what it was in the Middle Ages, as being to a large extent a change in the way her influence takes effect. This does not mean that we should always meekly accept the collapse of the traditional forms: that by no means follows. What does follow is this: that whenever any forms of her influence disappear against our own will and despite all we do, we are still far from being lost, because the fact is that her influence can go on existing and be won back again in new and different ways.

IV

And now finally let us take a look at these so-called "facts", which are supposed to be the reason for our despair. On the whole, Christianity and the Church seem to all intents and purposes to be on the defensive. Despite her partial successes in the missionary field, the Church seems to be on the down-grade, in a state of retreat, and the fight she is waging seems only to be prolonging the process, not halting it. When we look out upon the world as a whole, the general historical tendency seems to be that in terms of sheer numbers the Church is becoming simply another religious sect—though a big one—existing in a sort of *cul-de-sac,* in some dead corner of the world history of the future. Is this a simple fact, a fair estimate of the future, based on undeniable objective facts; or is it, not a fact, but a false or at least highly dubious interpretation of the facts?

To begin with, two theological dogmas must be remembered, if these "facts" are to be seen in the right perspective.

The first of these is the fact of our Lord's second coming, and the uncertainty as to when this is to be. This article of faith may seem ridiculous to the pagans and Christian de-mythologizers of our day, but it is one of the truths of faith, a truth to be remembered, a truth lodged firmly in our hearts. We do not know when the Lord will come—like lightning, and when unbelievers least expect him. We cannot say, "The time is miles away", and go on living as though there were no need to give a second thought to it. But so far as our present problem is concerned, this only brings out the dubiousness of the facts we find so disturbing. Are we really quite so sure what these facts really signify? Are they the beginning of a slow sickness that is bound to grow increasingly severe, and of a gradual atrophy of the Church's life whilst the world goes merrily on its way into new epochs, or do they denote the beginning of the final woes, the decay and death of love prophesied as heralding the end of time? Are they signs given us so that we shall not go astray when even the elect are in danger? Anyone who seriously believes in our Lord's second coming must by the very fact of his belief take the latter possibility into account. When this is done, the so-called facts assume quite a different complexion. Then the words *Ecce praedixi vobis*, the divine "Behold I have foretold it unto you", in which all the guilt and apostasy of all the ages is enfolded, apply in the most radical sense. The answer given by faith is then plainly, in spite of all the blindness of the world, the only thing that counts.

The second truth concerns the importance of grace in the matter of faith and election. A little dose of Jansenism would be no bad thing here. We are all too prone to think that God is under an obligation to offer the grace of faith and Church membership to everyone, and when we fail to see any effects of this grace we instinctively take it to be a sign not that something is wrong with human beings but that something is wrong with the Faith and the Church. The fact is that we should rather give thanks, as people quite undeservedly given the possibility of redemption, and marvel that one single heart is opened to God's grace, instead of being taken aback by the

65

fact that so many hearts seem to remain closed against it. We accept Christianity as a matter of course, and then are amazed to find that it is not accepted everywhere. If we were to see our Faith and the Church as what they really are, an absolute miracle of grace, an astonishing act of election, then we should be less appalled at finding this grace vouchsafed to so few. We could then, without disquiet, leave to God's own wisdom the question of how many people find ultimate bliss, for though he has enjoined on us that we are to seek our salvation through the means he has laid down for us, he has not so bound himself or his grace. If we saw things from this point of view there would be no need for us to be perturbed by the thought that in former days there were relatively more people who enjoyed the grace of believing in God and the Church than there are today. For in the last analysis belief in God and the Church is only of value if it leads to ultimate salvation. And it is quite fair to say that today anyone who has the grace of faith and practises his religion as a living reality is nearer to eternal salvation than he would have been in the old days. For more is demanded of the believer and done by him than was the case in former times.

Where salvation is concerned, what counts is the absolute, not the relative, number of people involved, for in this matter everyone is alone. But who knows: even if we have only twenty per cent of "practising" Catholics today, this is still in absolute terms far more than the presumed hundred per cent of earlier periods in the same epoch. Geniuses do not feel themselves to be in any danger just because there are so few of them. If we had, as a corollary to this, what we ought to have, a humbly proud consciousness of the ineffable degree to which we have been favoured by grace, if we really saw it as an infinite gift and not simply as imposing a duty upon us, we should not tend to look on ourselves as cutting no very impressive figure because, apparently, we form such a tiny flock. If only we would think of Christianity more as a grace, in which something is given to persons who can take hold of it, and not so much as something demanded of people reluctant to give it, then our words would often have more compelling power upon others.

After these theological observations, let us take a somewhat closer look at this present condition of Christianity which we find so disturbing, and regard it from a more empirical point of view. History is always in motion; there is never any end to it; one cannot finally point to it and say that one is outside it or that this is where it leaves off. It is not for nothing that world history, which does not include any idea of world judgement, is to be followed by a Judgement once it has come to an end. It is not for nothing that Christian behaviour is based on trust in God's inscrutable ways and judgements, on risk and trial. A period of history that seems—as it must—to the people experiencing and undergoing it to be a time of decline and catastrophe can look to later generations like an unavoidable transition period full of promise for the future. It was not by chance that Augustine and Gregory the Great saw their own day as a period of decline before the end of the world, when in fact it was something quite different, the dawn of a new —and yet everlastingly the same—kind of Christianity. If we had never known a mature human being, we might easily regard a period of religious crisis in a human being's adolescence as a pure catastrophe and the beginning of the end of all religious practices by the person concerned. Instead, we should see it as a transition period, accompanied perhaps by incidents of a regrettable or blameworthy kind, which may nevertheless be inevitable in the light of his whole life —the really important enduring element struggling to a new form through a period of apparent destruction. The meaning of any historical situation is a highly debatable thing so long as one remains exclusively within it, and if we sometimes feel with alarm that the facts under our very noses signify something like the beginning of the end of Christianity, then we have already given a highly debatable interpretation of these facts, not merely made a number of objective observations.

Now, there can be no doubt that today we are living in the midst of a transitional period of immense scope and depth. It is not for nothing that there has been talk of the end of the modern age. The day of European dominance in world affairs is over. The day of separate national histories, cut off from each other by areas of vast emptiness, is over too. The day of a unified world history has arrived. The fact that this one world is split into two is no argument against this, for the two parts are essentially involved with each other and can never again have their own independent destiny. Again, the day of technology has arrived. Human beings now live not according to nature but in a planned, ordered manner which they themselves have created and invented, to an extent unimaginable only a few centuries ago. Indeed, to a certain extent we now live according to a higher potential. And however much all these things may be only accidental changes judged by the standards of man's essentially metaphysical and hence religious nature, they are nevertheless of a depth that is at the moment beyond our power to appreciate—we probably tend to underestimate rather than to overestimate them. Chrysalis and butterfly are one and the same creature, yet what a transformation takes place when the one becomes the other! What a vast difference between the men of today and their forbears! The latter lived in a world of nature which they had made only superficially serviceable and remained essentially food-gatherers feeding upon her spontaneous products. The former, the new men who are now emerging, delve in confident mastery into nature's depths, even to the subatomic level, manufacture raw materials otherwise non-existent, land their rockets on the very face of the once-holy moon, and in all seriousness contemplate voyaging into space. The extent of a change so vast is no less than that between two different life stages in the same organism.

In a period like this it is not surprising that the whole of man's psychic life should be in a state of confusion and crisis, into which his religious life is sympathetically drawn. For this religious life of his is in a new context to which it has not yet managed to adapt itself. New, unexpected, as yet undisciplined impressions are invading the vast realms of his consciousness. Inevitably, for a time they force some of its other elements into the background. What we regard with such alarm as a symptom of the decline or degeneration of the religious nature in modern man is probably no more than the reflex, transposed into terms of the short-lived individual, of an adolescent crisis in the collective consciousness. This crisis may well continue for a long time, and hide the fact that the religious elements in man have merely been pushed into the background of the human consciousness. They will come to light again when man has surmounted the present crisis and become as much at home in his new world as he once was—and again it was a long process—in the world which we people of the transitional period are now leaving behind. When a young boy gets his first bicycle he may perhaps skip going to church for a few Sundays and go off on his own, because he can't think of anything but his new toy; but later, when it has become just an ordinary means of transport for him, he finds that it can also be used for riding *to* church on Sundays. Mankind's spiritual crisis will go on for more than a few Sundays, of course—in fact, for more than any of our individual lifetimes, and this is why it seems so endless to us Christians today, and why it constitutes such a threat to the personal salvation of all the individuals caught up in it. Nevertheless, it is at least not improbable that fundamentally the religious crisis of our day and age rests on the same simple psychic mechanism as the religious crisis of the young cyclist whose technical development has thoroughly upset his religious life for a while and taken away all his taste for religion (though not his religious propensities!).

If we look upon the present day in this way, then the question arises—in the unexistential sense alone open to us after what has been said above: Is there any real danger that the Church and Christianity, as a world religion plain for all to see, will not survive the present period of crisis in the human consciousness? This question can be answered with a firm No, even though none of us now alive will experience the truth of it in his own lifetime. To substantiate such a firm negative, which is made on the basis not of faith but of a purely secular consideration of human history and philosophy, two things are worth remembering. The first is man's indestructible religious propensity; the second, the empirical fact that Christianity—quite apart from any question of its truth or falsehood—has no formidable rival.

Man's religious instinct is indestructible. We can allow ourselves a deduction of a transcendental kind from this statement. Man is a spiritual being. No matter how exclusively he may have concentrated his spirituality during the last few centuries on mastering the material world—and so wasted it—he has at the same time given proof of its existence in the most incontrovertible way. Never was the factual—and at the same time empirically verifiable—disparity between man on the one hand, and nature and the animal world on the other, so great as it is today. It might almost be said that now for the first time man was beginning to give tangible proof of his essential being as something outside and beyond nature. Sooner or later, however (and in my opinion only, to any great extent, later), such a spiritual being is bound to inquire about the essence and meaning of his existence —not only his own as an individual but also mankind's collectively: and not only about the technical mastery of the isolated moments of his existence, either. This at once raises the religious question. At the same time the whole of human existence has lost some of its savour, and become harsher, more fraught with responsibility and danger, in spite of all man's dazzling "progress". It has already been shown that the apparent disturbance of his religious propensities does nothing to disprove this statement. Man, now just settled into his new world, has only to make himself at home again, to develop a lively sense of the finite and problematical nature of this new world of his—and this, it must be realized, has become greater, not less—and then the religious question will in all probability arise again, in the midst of all the modern methods of technology and mass leadership, to a degree and extent hardly imaginable today. As long as wireless and telescopes are interesting in themselves, human beings, being childlike and childish as they are, can't be bothered about what they see or hear through them: they are quite satisfied with the mere fact that the things work; but once they have got used to them and assimilated them psychologically, they will find out how to use them in such a way as to see and hear something of real value through them.

But when this time comes along, the glad tidings of Christianity will once again be the only answer to mankind's newly resuscitated aspirations. For to begin with, it is a surprising fact, though not at all apparent at first sight, that there is no new religion on the horizon of the new era as the answer to mankind's religious potential, and it is quite fair to say that for the first time in history a new era will be arising without a new religion to go along with it. Communism tries to provide man's religious aspirations with an objective rooted in this world. But this attempt has behind it an ideological impulse so primitive and outmoded that it is bound to fail in the end, no matter how much naked force it can call upon. Nor is this all: once the objective has been attained—the objective which never goes beyond this world, and to which mankind's religious dynamism has been harnessed—once the goal has been reached, the classless society, the earthly paradise, or at least some comparatively stable and lasting order of society corresponding to the new technological situation— man's religious energy will inevitably demand a fresh outlet. Once again, once the problems relating only to this world have been solved, the transcendental problem of meaning will arise;

73

for man will again find himself a finite creature with the problem of the infinite on his mind, a mortal being hankering after immortality. But there is no new religion in these modern days of ours that seems likely to set itself up in competition with Christianity. Less than at any time in its history has Christianity a serious rival. All the former historical religions have on the purely empirical level already lost their battle with Christianity, no matter what they are called: Mohammedanism, Hinduism, Buddhism, or anything else you like. Thus the only sort of person who can have any serious doubts about Christianity's chances in the long run is the kind of person who believes—like the Communist, who in this respect is a rationalist out of the backwoods of the nineteenth century, not a truly modern man—that man's whole religious sense is on the way out.

Furthermore, we have only to make clear to ourselves, even if we are unbelievers, what characteristics could qualify a religion to compete with Christianity, to be convinced that the appearance of such a vital religion cannot even be imagined.

Such a religion would have to be in the first place a transcendental one; it would have to show mankind some way out of this world. And it would have to do this more successfully than ever. For the more completely man subjugates this world, only to find himself the same anxious, limited and mortal being with the same craving for the infinite, the more utterly profane must the world become; the more incapable of investiture with the unearthly radiance of holiness and mystery, of providing an object of worship. Nor will he be able to persist indefinitely in worshipping himself. This will, in fact, be more difficult than ever before. For all progress is at bottom a clearer understanding of man's inner limitation, experience of his problematical situation. The fact that Russian peasants, now for the first time waking up in amazement to the possibilities of technology and world domination, should not yet recognize this, is no argument against this estimate of the future.

No religion in the unified world and unified world history of today and the future can afford to be regionally tied, as merely the reflex of one particular history or one particular nation. Christianity has already proved itself in principle a religion for mankind as a whole. This universality is now becoming more evident than ever in the past. Perhaps its non-European origin will gain a new and positive significance with the shift of the world's centre of gravity from Europe, possibly in the direction of Asia.

In the days to come a religion will need to be highly realistic; it will need to have something to say about the darker side of life, for there will still be such a thing as death in A.D. 2000 and A.D. 2100, and death will still be as desperately bitter a thing as it is now, even in the clinics of A.D. 2100, despite all the developments in medical technique that will have taken place and all the artificial screens that will have been erected against these deeper layers of human existence.

Lastly, a religion will have to be historical. It is precisely the man of the future, making and knowing and organizing everything himself, who will long with an elemental longing for something not made, something unquestionable, something handed down to him, something that has always been in existence; not something thought up artificially and settled in a Politburo and worked out for a purpose by the rational human mind. Precisely because he will no longer, or hardly ever, find anything of this kind in any all-controlling "divine" Nature, with an ever-recurring cycle of events, he will search for it with all the more elemental an impulse in his religion, and long for a faith that has not been put together in his own day by a handful of gifted brains but has always existed, one that comes down in an unbroken historical line from a beginning plain for all eyes to see. People whose whole life is, as it were, "prefabricated", and have to accept this as their destiny, will not want to have anything to do with a synthetic religion. The thing they will find most modern in this condition of things will be something as old as the hills.

But where and how could such a new religion arise, transcendental, universal, realistic and historically mature? How could it possibly compete with a religion that has the audacity to say that it is the word of the living God, coming down from beyond this world with a promise of other-worldly eternity, a religion that is already universal, a religion originating from both Europe and Asia—the religion of the Cross, the most historical religion of all, the oldest religion in the world? .

And even if it has to be also a religion for supermen, Christianity has always been the religion of the God-Man in such a breath-taking sense that it is as though endless spaces are opened out in it, in which man's Promethean *hubris*, only now coming into the open, alone can develop sensibly and slowly. And if latter-day Western individualism is coming to an end, and a feeling of general collectivism is on the upsurge, then the religion of love, of the Kingdom of God, of the Church, of the unity of all mankind in guilt and redemption, need have no fear. And if man the individualist, as he was until recently, has to go through the fire of collectivism now burning on both sides of the Iron Curtain, then he will have small desire left to fashion a private personal philosophy of his own for his private satisfaction, like the men of the nineteenth century. Nor will he be prepared to take his philosophy from any Ministry of Propaganda. He will want it from a Church, a wise old Church, a Church grown kind but firm in its lovingkindness. No; even if we take only the factors of this world into account, we may be sure that if there is to be any religion in the future, it will be the Christian religion.

v

What follows from what has been said, so far as we ourselves and our special duty of helping to spread the Christian message are concerned?

If, taking the situation as a whole, mankind is living through a critical *Sturm und Drang* period, then whatever religious impulse still remains to it cannot be expected to lead to any sudden reflowering of Christianity and the Church. Now, I am no prophet, and I am quite ready to learn from experience that there are more grounds for optimism than I have imagined and that God's benevolent grace has bigger and better surprises in store for us in the relatively near future than seems likely at the moment. But pending that I cannot see much possibility of a new "Christian era", of any appreciable or fundamental improvement in our position as Christians and members of the Christian Church, within the foreseeable future. A train of thought, with a consequent forecast of events, can take place in our own minds in a few seconds, but in the mind of society at large, in the real actuality of things, this train of thought may in certain circumstances take centuries to work itself out. And so our ideas may be absolutely right in a general sort of way and yet their realization in actual history may still take a long time, despite the speed with which historical events are taking place today in both the intellectual and the collective spheres.

We Christians of today shall probably therefore spend the rest of our lives in the depressing situation with which this essay has been concerned. We shall remain on the defensive. We shall most likely see a further decline of faith on the empirical level, and of the practice of religion and the influence of the Church as we have so far known it. We shall feel as though we are living amongst people thoroughly opaque to religion, talking to deaf ears and uncomprehending hearts. Perhaps political changes may make things considerably worse, until we reach a stage when our very existence is threatened. All this is possible and indeed probable, even though our hopes for the ultimate prospects of Christianity —even seen from the point of view of this world alone—are justified.

Our position, in fact, is rather like that of front-line soldiers in the middle of a battle. They may know that the battle has already been won, but their own position at any particular moment, as they lie in their dug-outs under fierce enemy fire, is nevertheless decidedly grim. What we have to do is to show the patience and grim determination of men determined to fight on. We have no reason to harbour feelings of defeatism in our hearts, as though the final victory were in question. But we shall not manage to avoid a period of dogged self-defence, in the immediate present and for a long time to come.

Yet our position is not such that it does not matter whether we fight on or not, as though, however poor our chances now, final victory were in the long run assured. A careful study of spiritual matters shows that even in the same general conditions of race and civilization, social and intellectual background, the final results of the spiritual ministration of the priesthood and efforts of laypeople who co-operate with them, can vary considerably. The deciding factor is whether they do their work in a spirit of devotion, self-sacrifice, holiness, penance and sincere prayer, or whether even the most essential and official duties are performed slackly, mechanically and as matters of official routine. Thus, even though we are at present on the defensive, we can still be aiming at very different objects, according to the degree of our goodwill. It will depend to a very great extent on us and what we do today, whether in time to come, when offensive action is again possible, the Church is able to utilize the new situation to the full. Though we are on the defensive now, we may be fighting for a victory that will settle the issue for centuries. One man sows and another reaps.

When I say that it is our duty and present destiny to be on the defensive, I do not of course mean that we are only to try to preserve whatever there is still left to preserve. In this matter, as in many others, attack is the best defence, and even though any attack we may make may only aim at a passing tactical success which in no wise alters the defensive nature of our position as bearers of the Christian message, it still remains true that the man who can best defend himself is the man who has the courage to attack. One person newly won over by missionary endeavour from a society now returned to its original paganism is worth more from the missionary point of view than three times as many who have simply hung on from the old Christian dispensation; for they or their children will probably be lost later, since, never having passed through the crisis of their day, they have not been immunized against the spirit of the age and are all too likely to have no resistance to its infection. Even in such purely local offensive moves, actual tangible numerical success is not the prime essential. The mere courage to embark on such offensive action and win over a handful of converts can mean a great deal, sometimes everything. At the start the result may seem disappointingly small, but in the end it may prove to have been a victory fraught with absolutely unforeseeable consequences. When Saint Benedict arrived at Monte Cassino with a handful of monks to establish the monastic way of life there he little realized that he was to be the founder of a new Western world.

Soldiers win victories not through being certain that they are going to win through in the end, but by being ready to die in battle for their country, even though they can see no future in it for themselves. One might perhaps imagine a herd of animals fighting in the former way; but never human beings. Similarly, the Christian of today will not only fight on in a spirit of grim, patient determination because he is convinced that in the end absolute victory will be his and in the less distant future relative victories will come for those things for which he is struggling and sacrificing himself; he must be capable of absolute faith and absolutely selfless love. He must feel in his bones that he will one day have to give an account of himself before the judgement seat of God with no one there to help and support him, stating whether or not he was faithful to the duties of his day, duties which he was not free to choose. He must know that he will not be dispensed from thus appearing before God and his judgement and his eternal love simply because the duty laid upon him is a hard one and the times are dark and death is near. If we ourselves did not so often think and feel in such a purely worldly and sheepish way, if we felt more strongly in our bones that we stand or fall by God alone, then the contention of our times and any temporary lack of success we might experience would never meet with anything other than brave and believing hearts.